Senedd

Welsh Parliament building designed by Richard Rogers, words by Trevor Fishlock, photographs by Andrew Molyneux

GRAFFEG

Trevor Fishlock

Writer and broadcaster Trevor Fishlock reported Wales for *The Times* in the 1970s, wrote from more than sixty countries as a foreign correspondent, was *The Times* correspondent in India and New York, and *The Daily Telegraph* bureau chief in Moscow. He won the International Reporter of the Year prize in the British Press Awards.

He has written and presented 130 television programmes on life, history and landscape in Wales, including the long-running *Wild Tracks* for which he won a Bafta. He is the author of books about Wales, India, America and Russia. His *Conquerors of Time* is a narrative of nineteenth-century world exploration and *In This Place* is the story of Wales commissioned by the National Library of Wales as its centenary volume. A taste for salt water led him to sail twice across the North Atlantic and also across the Southern Ocean from Cape Town to Melbourne. He lives in Cardiff.

Andrew Molyneux

Andrew was born in Cardiff in 1963 and spent his early years carrying his father Colin's tripod around the country. Graduating from tripod carrier to full time assistant for Colin, he learned everything he knows about photography from the best teacher he could have, his dad. He went on to work as an assistant to some of the best corporate photographers in the USA.

On returning to this country he gained a reputation as a creative corporate photographer, working for many of the top FTSE 100 companies. His work over the last thirty years has taken him all over the world photographing a huge range of subjects.

For the people

The Welsh Parliament (Welsh: Senedd Cymru)
is the elected body representing the people
of Wales. It makes laws for Wales and holds
the Welsh government to account. The Welsh
Parliament has sixty elected Members of the
Senedd, MSs, and is the equivalent in Wales to
the United Kingdom parliament at Westminster.
Voters elect the Welsh Parliament every five
years.

The Welsh Government is distinct from
the Welsh Parliament and is the devolved
Government for Wales. It consists of the First
Minister, the Welsh ministers, the Counsel
General and deputy ministers, fifteen people in
all. It works to improve the lives of the people
of Wales and is supported by civil servants
in the key devolved responsibilities of health,
education and the environment. It has offices
in Merthyr Tydfil, Aberystwyth and Llandudno
Junction.

The word *senedd* derives from the Latin
synodus, meeting together, which has altered
slightly under the influence of the Latin
senatus, a council of elders.

Contents

01 Introduction

Daring lends grace to the Senedd in the Bay. Classic lines and curves shape a forum of exhilarating space and clarity. Inside and out a sense of promenade prevails. Agored is the apt Welsh word here: openness. Imagine it expressed with outstretched arms.

The home of the Welsh Parliament, originally known as the National Assembly for Wales, is a first in history, a political and architectural landmark growing naturally from the story of Wales and the accretions and aspirations of the political nation.

The Assembly design competition asked architects to bear in mind the country's cultural individuality and historical hinterland. In his introduction to the design brief Lord Callaghan wrote that the contest offered 'the opportunity to express a concept of a democratic Assembly listening to and leading a small democratic nation'. He hoped the chosen construction would become 'a visible symbol, recognised and respected throughout the world whenever the name of Wales is used'.

Lord Callaghan's shrewd words made a difference. The winning Richard Rogers team adopted them as an inspirational spur. Lord Rogers and Ivan Harbour, the partner responsible for the Senedd, envisaged a gathering place and created a building whose form follows function and frames a simple and spirited democratic workshop.

Transparency and accessibility proclaim the ideal of a listening leadership in a peopled place.

The Senedd is a national institution. It is also an artistic achievement. Elegance puts rhythm in its step. It engages with its surroundings. The curvilinear roof creating a portico beyond the glass front is imagined as an extension of the sky. The swells of the sculpted ceiling lift every visitor's chin. The ensemble of glass, steel, slate and timber play in a drama of space and light in the confluence of all the voices of Wales.

Someone has scribbled in the visitors' book the single word: 'Stunnin'.'

The Assembly insisted that the structure should be efficiently green and energy-mean: fanned, fuelled, flushed, warmed, cooled, lit and watered the twenty-first century way. Natural is the watchword and the emphasis is on daylight and fresh air.

The Senedd building overlooking Cardiff Bay, adventurous, classical and made in Wales.

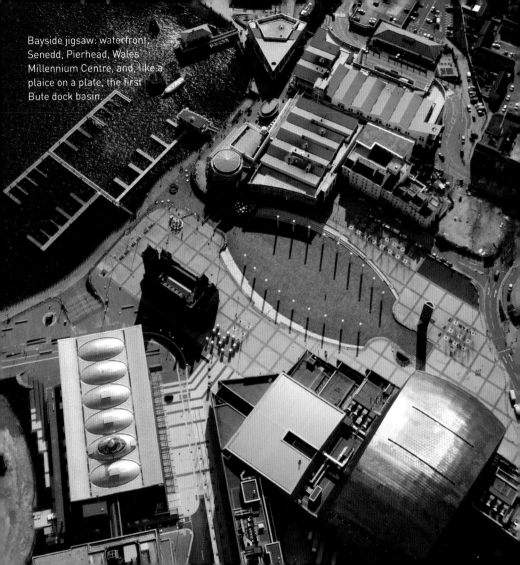

Bayside jigsaw: waterfront Senedd, Pierhead, Wales Millennium Centre, and, like a plaice on a plate, the first Bute dock basin.

On the upper floor the spectacular cedarwood funnel rising to the flowing ceiling suggests a village meeting place, under a banyan tree perhaps. A glass collar at its base, a stroke of puckish genius, allows visitors a glimpse into the digitally-streamlined Siambr below where Members of the Senedd vote in an electronic instant.

The human scale of this ideas exchange corresponds with Winston Churchill's musings on the most comfortable setting for parliamentary discussion. 'A small chamber and a sense of intimacy,' he once noted, 'are indispensable.'

In the story of Wales the Senedd stands at a point of arrival and departure, the end of one journey and the beginning of another. One meaning of this stimulating place is a broader acceptance of responsibility. That itself derives from the people's deepening self-respect. What happens here must fulfil the purpose for which the Senedd was created. Decision will be increasingly in the hands of the people of Wales.

Only a few years ago the spectacle we see today, the Senedd as the keystone in the astonishing transformation of Cardiff Bay, lay in the realm of hope and dream.

The catalytic outcome of the 1997 referendum on devolved government set the ball rolling. The preamble to the Government of Wales Act in 1998 said simply: Bydd Cynulliad i Gymru. There shall be an Assembly for Wales.

The following year the Queen opened the National Assembly in its temporary chamber in the Crickhowell House administration block, now renamed Tŷ Hywel. In 2000 engineers completed the Cardiff Bay barrage dam, impounding the estuaries of the Taff and Ely rivers, so that Cardiff's tidal shores and whaleback mudflats were lost from view beneath a freshwater lake of 500 acres. In 2004 the Wales Millennium Centre for arts and opera raised the curtain on its musical life. In 2006 the Queen inaugurated the new Senedd building which completed the jigsaw of waterfront buildings in the eastern curve of the Bay.

Apart from its national and political function the Senedd is a destination for visitors. On its acropolis of mountain slate it faces the south-western horizon and the prevailing wind. It draws on the sea and sky. From its front piazza and through its crystal wall there is the prospect of Cardiff Bay, Penarth Head, Saint Augustine's church, the dam and the Severn Sea beyond.

This is fitting. The sea is there to ponder on. Wales is an Atlantic country of long maritime tradition and three quarters of its border is defined by salt water. The Senedd rises at a famous junction of coal and ocean where a city and a history were made. From this promontory Wales looks the world in the eye.

Side by side and a century apart: Pierhead Building 1897, Senedd 2006, Victorian pomp and ultra-modern clarity perform their architectural drama.

Waterfront witness: the Pierhead Building and changing times. Cardiff Bay barrage, top; Tŷ Hywel, Senedd and old East Dock entrance, left; Wales Millennium Centre; West Dock entrance and basin; Saint David's hotel, centre; Butetown Link crosses River Taff, top right.

02 Background

The brief for the Senedd design competition noted that the new political structure in Wales was not strictly a renascence but a genesis. There is certainly a tradition of renewal against the odds. The story of Wales is one of a national persistence, remaking and tenacity over 1600 years.

Wales and the Welsh language emerged in the aftermath of Rome's fourth-century retreat from Britain. In the seventh century its people called themselves Cymry, or fellow countrymen. Their Saxon neighbours knew them as Welsh, meaning people different from themselves. The eighth-century English king Offa raised the dyke signifying Wales's eastern frontier. In the tenth century King Hywel Dda consolidated Welsh laws, a mark of nationhood.

The Normans swiftly conquered England and gentle lowland Wales and took two centuries to subdue mountain Wales. In this interlude the culture of Welsh princes bloomed. Late in the eleventh century a cleric gathered the eleven fantastic prose tales of the Mabinogion from the tongues of storytellers and preserved them in ink.

Owain Glyn Dŵr raised national awareness in his revolt against English rule and people of all sorts flocked to his flag. His struggle peaked in 1404-5 and English attrition broke him. Centuries later he assumed the mantle of national hero.

Henry VIII's laws of 1536 and 1542 made Wales and England an equal entity and declared English the language of government. Wales sent its first MPs to London in 1542. At a crucial time for their language scholars secured an Act of Parliament in 1563 commanding a Welsh Bible. William Morgan's translation of 1588 flowed as a linguistic and literary stream. From the 1730s Griffith Jones's roaming Bible teachers spread literacy to thousands of families.

Since no town in eighteenth-century Wales was large enough to support a tribe of Welsh writers and arguers, literary creativity prospered in London where Welsh groups congregated in lively debate and learning. From the 1760s Richard Price, a Presbyterian minister-philosopher from Llangeinor, Glamorgan, championed liberty, encouraged Americans in their independence struggle and declared every civil society's right to self-government.

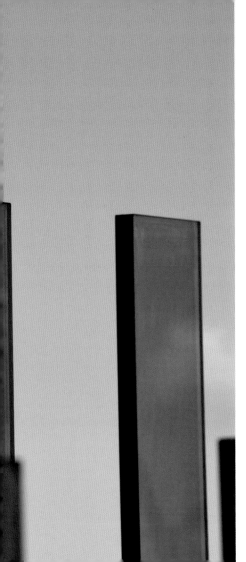

A growing Welsh consciousness encouraged campaigns for institutions from the 1840s and invigorated Welsh literature, journalism and publishing. The song 'Hen Wlad fy Nhadau', written by Evan and James James in Pontypridd in 1856, became the national anthem. Welsh money built the university at Aberystwyth in 1872. The National Eisteddfod established itself as the chief literary festival. The University of Wales took root in 1893, the Welsh Rugby Union in 1899, the National Library in 1907 and the National Museum in 1908.

Chartism, liberalism and socialism grew muscular in Wales. The 1867 voting reform gave a voice to oppressed farmers and workers. The election in 1868 of the nonconformist MP Henry Richard emphasised the influence of dissent in Welsh politics and society. The Liberal parliamentary majority in Wales lasted from 1868 to 1922. Lloyd George's ascent from the 1890s bolstered Welsh feelings of political equality with England.

Welsh skills and ingenuity played a large part in British industrial expansion and expertise. Two-thirds of the people of Wales lived in the industrial districts of Glamorgan and Monmouthshire. In sixty years from 1851 360,000 Welsh-speaking people from rural Wales joined the coal rush and with English, Irish, Italian and other incomers created a remarkable society.

Labour won twenty-five of thirty-six Welsh seats in 1945. Until the 1960s political debate in Wales turned on industrial and social concerns. Like Lloyd George in his day Aneurin Bevan and James Griffiths were key Welsh figures in founding the welfare state.

Winston Churchill created a Welsh section in the Home Office in 1951. Cardiff was designated capital of Wales in 1955. In 1964 prime minister Harold Wilson established the cabinet post of secretary of state for Wales with James Griffiths its first holder. The creation of the Welsh Office recognized a territorial unity in Wales. Trade unionists founded TUC Wales in 1973. Cardiff grew as a political centre.

The 1961 census showing a fall in the number of Welsh-speakers to 26 per cent of the population precipitated the language campaign of the 1960s and 1970s.

Legislation and practice, signs, documents and advertising, have changed the face of Wales in the past forty years, giving the country a bilingual public appearance to which commerce and institutions, banks, stores and other enterprises contribute. Demand for bilingual schools increased significantly. Broadcasting in Welsh has grown stronger. In 1977 BBC radio broadcasting was divided linguistically between Radio Wales and Radio Cymru. The Welsh television channel S4C started in 1982. Broadcasting in general has both stimulated and reflected the development of Welsh politics. Similarly the cadre of historians responds to, and encourages, a widening interest in Wales and its story.

Wales rejected devolution proposals in 1979. Debate continued. In the 1997 referendum the popular New Labour government and large numbers of younger people backed a National Assembly. Almost two decades of European Union membership changed the political context of devolution. The miners' defeat in the bitter strike of 1984-5 strengthened the mood for change. A 30 per cent swing in the Yes vote delivered a majority of 6,721 votes and an Assembly for Wales with limited powers. The Assembly first sat in 1999 and gained law-making powers in the Government of Wales Act 2006. In May 2008 the National Assembly agreed its first Assembly Measure. This was the first Welsh law passed in Wales since the time of Hywel Dda in the tenth century.

1x
1999–2009

The first decade: marking
the democratic milestone.

03 First city

Cardiff's Victorian accelerando established it as the first city of Wales. Its twentieth-century consolidation as capital and European city, focus of government, business and education, made it the pole to which the compass needle turned. On the edge of the twenty-first century it was the natural home of the Welsh Parliament.

In English and in Welsh, Cardiff and Caerdydd, the name means the fort on the Taff. The Romans raised a wooden fort in the first century to command the river crossing. In the fourth century new walls enclosed nine acres and in 1081 William the Conqueror ordered a timber fortress built among the Roman stones. A century later the Norman ruler of Cardiff raised the twelve-sided limestone keep we see today.

For most of the 750 years between Norman conquest and Victorian surge Cardiff's people numbered around 2,000. The Black Death reduced the town and Owain Glyn Dŵr besieged it. The Civil War apart, it mostly lived quietly, trading corn, butter, sheep and salt to Bristol and Somerset. Its destiny, though, lay with the industrial volcano. In the landmark year of 1798 Merthyr Tydfil's ironmasters completed a twenty-five mile canal to the Taff estuary at Cardiff. They sent down barges loaded with iron and, increasingly and significantly, with coal. Surveys in the 1820s told the second marquess of Bute of the immense coal wealth beneath his south Wales lands. Seeing the limitations of the canal he built his great dock of 1839 to ship out iron and coal in bulk.

In 1851 the admiralty chose Welsh steam coal for its new warships. It burned very hot and made little smoke to smudge the horizon. The Royal Navy's choice helped create a world market and the Butes opened more docks in 1859, 1874 and 1877. By 1860 three-fifths of Welsh coal went abroad. The very word 'Cardiff' on the cargo guaranteed higher prices.

Coal trains ran day and night and marshalling yards grew vast as Cardiff and the coalfield became a global energy capital. The Rhondda valleys were the most intensively-mined district on earth. Cardiff meanwhile multiplied from 20,000 people in 1851 to 160,000 in 1901 and enjoyed the boom-town accolade of 'the Welsh Chicago'.

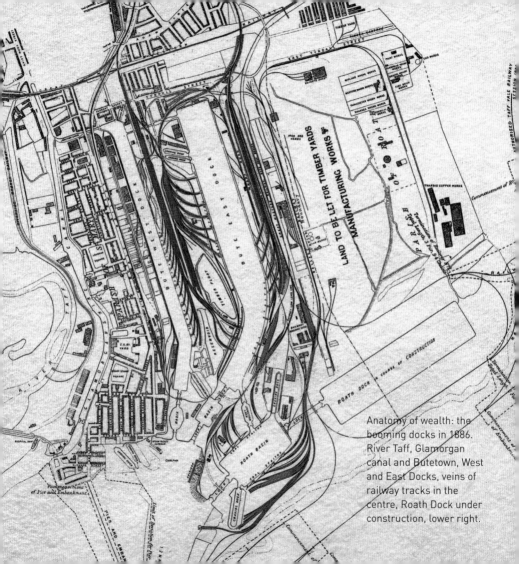

Anatomy of wealth: the booming docks in 1886. River Taff, Glamorgan canal and Butetown, West and East Docks, veins of railway tracks in the centre, Roath Dock under construction, lower right.

'Salt-caked smoke stack': coasters waiting to load coal in the West Dock below the Pierhead Building, 1930s.

As a source of wages and excitement coal provided an alternative to Atlantic emigration and helped to keep Welsh families and Welshness in Wales. The monumental Cardiff Coal and Shipping Exchange opened in 1886 as the arena where shouting dealers fixed the British and international price of coal. Here in 1907 the world's first cheque for a million pounds was written, equivalent to around £90 million today.

In the meantime, in 1898, Cardiff council bought fifty-nine acres of Cathays Park from the third marquess of Bute for £160,000. Here it laid out the loveliest civic centre in Britain. The baroque masterpiece of the city hall, designed by Lanchester, Stewart and Rickards, shone with the confidence of the age and set a standard for aldermanic Edwardian buildings. Grand and gleaming in Portland stone, framed by avenues, lawns and roses, the Cathays buildings included the Law Courts, National Museum, County Hall and University College. Thus Cathays Park gave birth to the soubriquet 'the Welsh Washington', a brother for 'the Welsh Chicago'.

King Edward VII came to Cardiff in 1905 and awarded it city status, a municipal peerage affirming its significance as the chief metropolis of Wales. As it happened, many of its pragmatic shipping and coal barons cared nothing for Wales and little for Cardiff, their main interest being money, not social leadership.

War delivery: a Hurricane fighter at Cardiff Docks in 1942.

The coal trade in Cardiff peaked in the year before the First World War. The world-wide resonance of the city's name was reflected in the title of Eugene O'Neill's play, *Bound East for Cardiff*, about a dying seaman. It was produced in America in 1916. After the war Cardiff and the valleys hinterland paid heavily for dependence on mining and export. A post-war shipping boom was short-lived. Oil began to supplant coal. From 1925 economic depression ground away at work, life and dignity in the valleys. But Cardiff had a city's momentum and resilience, the means to replenish itself.

It expanded as a business and shopping hub, a place for light industry and the natural base of institutions, colleges and administrative headquarters.

The Bute family quit in 1947 and gave the city their castle and liberating acres of riverside parkland and avenues of trees stretching to Llandaff. In 1955 the Queen confirmed the obvious fact and named Cardiff the capital of Wales. From the 1960s the city grew as a political and administrative hub and the base for national organizations, educators, broadcasters, media businesses and cultural bodies.

Internal migration has made Cardiff much more a city of Wales. Many young people have decided that, with its universities, school of medicine, colleges, social opportunities, employment and entertainment, this was the place where they wished to study, work and live. Their presence has made Cardiff livelier, more energetic, more attractive and more Welsh in spirit. In 1998 Ron Davies, the secretary of state for Wales, cited 'compelling reasons' for building the Senedd in Cardiff. One was that Wales had invested forty years in promoting the city as the country's capital. In Britain and in Europe the former fort by the river speaks for Wales. In short, Cardiff counts.

Moving energy: coal wagons crowd a marshalling yard near Roath Dock in March 1927.

Makers of Cardiff

More than any city in Britain Cardiff bears the dominant imprint of one man. John Crichton-Stuart, second marquess of Bute, created his own industrial revolution and transformed Cardiff into an energy metropolis. The wealth he derived from coal, docks and railways made his family fabulously rich. A quarter of the people of Wales live on former Bute land.

The Butes were Scots who married Welsh and English money and figured large in Cardiff life from 1766 to 1947. The second marquess was twenty-one when he inherited the estates in 1814. Although infrequently in Wales he ran them through copious correspondence, much of it with his agent who was also town clerk of Cardiff. He sent six letters a day for twenty-five years and dictated most of them because his myopia rendered him half-blind. Meanwhile, he gave time to philanthropy and the anti-slavery cause. Visiting Cardiff from his beloved Scotland he stayed in his castle and ordered his dinners sent over from the Cardiff Arms hotel.

He ventured the huge sum of £350,000 to build the Bute West Dock, the greatest engineering project of its kind in the world, opened in October 1839. On his death in 1848 his son, the third marquess, became the wealthiest one-year-old in Britain. He grew up shy and

Mystic marquess: John Patrick Crichton-Stuart, 1847-1900, Cardiff colourist, passionate builder, hero of Disraeli's novel *Lothair*, third marquess of Bute.

Right: Gull's-eye view: Pierhead Building presides over the West Dock on the left.

studious, something of a mystic, with none of his father's interest in business. He converted to Roman Catholicism, bought land in Palestine and spent lavishly on Cardiff castle. Here he and the artist-architect William Burges brought a dream to life and created a unique and brilliant medievalist masterpiece in glorious colour. It was the most magnificent assignment of Burges's career. A statue of Lord Bute's father, the second marquess, stands in Callaghan Square facing north to the valleys, as if acknowledging the source of all the family's wealth.

Gull's eye view:
Pierhead Building
presides over the West
Dock on the left, the
East Dock entrance
where the Senedd now
stands, lower right.

'we were received by my
own Welsh friends and endowed
with all good things'

Edward Evans, navigation officer

Cardiff farewell

Captain Robert Scott's South Pole expedition ship *Terra Nova* called at Cardiff for coal in June 1910. 'We were received by my own Welsh friends and endowed with all good things,' wrote Edward Evans, the young navigating officer. 'Free docking, free coal, defects made good for nothing, everything done with open-hearted generosity.'

Businessmen dined Scott and his officers at the Royal Hotel on 13 June. The city leaders who toured the ship in Roath Dock earned a disdainful note in the diary of Captain Oates, the cavalry officer who perished with Scott. 'The Mayor and his crowd came on board and I never saw such a mob – they are Labour Socialists.' Cardiff gave *Terra Nova* a tremendous send-off on 15 June. 'Thousands yelled as if they had taken leave of their senses,' wrote Tryggve Gran, a Norwegian member of the expedition. 'Railway wagons were rolled over a line covered with dynamite detonators, and vessels in their hundreds completed the noise with whistles and sirens.' *Terra Nova* hoisted the Welsh flag and set sail and Edward Evans recalled 'a rattling good time in Cardiff'. Scott left the ship soon after it sailed to do some more fundraising and rejoined it in New Zealand. He and his four companions

Above: Free coal: Lieutenant Edward Evans and Captain Scott aboard *Terra Nova* at Cardiff. Evans won fame in 1917 commanding HMS *Broke* in action against German warships.

Left: To the earth's ends: *Terra Nova*, wooden three-masted barque, 749 tons, built 1884, leaves Cardiff in 1910 on her second Antarctic voyage. She sank off Greenland in 1943.

reached the Pole on 17 January 1912 and died on the return journey.

Terra Nova returned to Cardiff in 1913 and was met by Lady Scott and her son Peter. The ship's binnacle, the compass housing, is in the Pierhead Building. In Jonathan Williams's sculpture on the Bay waterfront Scott hauls a sled, leaning defiantly into a blizzard, the faces of his companions locked in the snow. The memorial stands by the old lock through which *Terra Nova* departed.

Norwegian Church

Something of the fjord: the corrugated iron sailors' church in its original setting, 1955.

The Norwegian church is a reminder of the large part played in Cardiff's fortunes by thousands of Scandinavian and other foreign seamen. It was built and consecrated in 1868 between the West and East Docks. Its services, reading room, Scandinavian newspapers and pictures of Norwegian scenes made it a popular rendezvous. The infant Roald Dahl, born in Cardiff, the son of an Oslo shipbroker, was baptized in the church in 1916. The church closed in 1974 but was rebuilt with money raised in Wales and Norway and reopened as a cafe and meeting place.

'And so we were docked at last; and all the sharks, butchers, tailors, compass-adjustors and candlestick-makers of Cardiff came aboard until it was difficult to move about the decks, and customs men with watery eyes drink what is left of the Old Man's whisky and harass and torment the personnel and the ship.

Smoke belches at us from the steamers moored all around, and men in brassbound uniforms shriek and shout orders through megaphones, and trains rattle over bridges, and coal dust fills the air, and idlers troop down in their hundreds to gaze up at the gauntness of the sail-stripped yards in wide-eyed wonder, and gape and say they would sooner be dead than sail in such a ship as ours.'

Alan Villiers, *Voyage of the Parma*, 1932.

Four-masted steel barque *Parma*, 3,091 tons, photographed by Alan Villiers at Cardiff in 1932, after sailing a cargo of grain from Australia to Britain.

Bute West Dock, early twentieth century.

Tiger Bay

The Cardiff sailortown known as Tiger Bay occupied the streets, squares and lanes between Bute Street and the Glamorgan canal. No one knows the origin of the name. There were other Tiger Bays in London and in Georgetown, Guyana. Perhaps Georgetown sailors brought the name to Cardiff. Perhaps it was a wry commentary on the unruliness of the seamen, pubs and gambling and opium dens.

From the 1850s this part of Cardiff was a world village drawing seafarers from Scandinavia, Russia, the Baltic countries, Italy, Spain, Malta, India, China, Malaya, Yemen, West Africa, Somalia and the Caribbean. Only London had a higher proportion of foreign-born inhabitants.

The name of Tiger Bay appeared on no maps. Butetown was its more formal name. It covered a square mile and its heyday ran from the 1870s to the 1920s. Race riots scarred the year 1919. In the nature of things seamen were often wanderers and men apart, but many settled and married in Cardiff and helped to create a distinct and varied Welsh community which gradually dispersed as the old dockland became derelict and, from the 1960s, was redeveloped. Tiger Bay vanished but a nostalgia for its life and times persists in pictures, pubs and picaresque stories.

Above: Bonnets, boaters and bowlers, plus sailorsuit and guitar: a Cardiff horse-bus outing in the old Bay days.

04

Challenge and concept

Birth of an idea: a few strokes and dots make architect Ivan Harbour's concept Senedd doodle. The building rises from the waterfront at right. The floating roof is sketched in with the funnel of light and air at left and the debating chamber below.

Fifty-five architects drawn to the international competition for the Senedd had to think hard. The brief called for more than a mere debating chamber. What was needed was the 'first ever national representative political institution', quite different from the parliament at Westminster, designed to make an immediate impact as the new political forum of Wales.

Lord Callaghan, the former prime minister, who chaired a judging panel of five lay people and two architectural advisers, wrote that the first elections for the National Assembly, in 1999, would signal the beginning of 'an epoch unique in the constitutional history of the nation'.

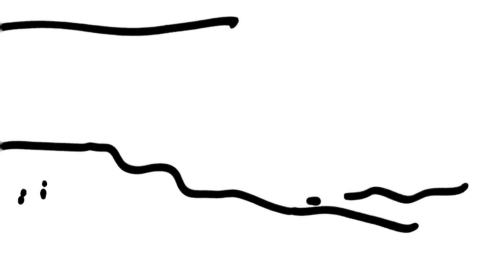

'the democratic process is made both transparent and approachable'

In October 1998 the judges considered a shortlist of six and chose the concept put forward by the Richard Rogers Partnership, now RSHP.

Ivan Harbour, the partner leading the project, drew the first key sketches of a glass hall poised between the sea and the sky, steps rising from the waterfront to a plinth, the whole transparent structure canopied by a sensational roof, a sequence of pleasing and accessible indoor and outdoor spaces. The building, he wrote, 'is firmly anchored to the water's edge, enabling it to establish an identity independent of the surrounding buildings … The terraces create spaces that will draw people into the building … In this way the democratic process is made both transparent and approachable.'

He also wrote a manifesto proposing an Assembly building that:

• Symbolizes democracy by encouraging public participation in the democratic process

• Is accessible because it is easy to understand

• Makes visible the workings of the Assembly

• Creates spaces with the minimum of walls and corridors

• Provides a protective environmental envelope

• Reduces energy consumption by maximizing use of daylight

• Engages with, and is open to, its surroundings

• Is a flexible concept that can accommodate change

• Is made secure by good planning

• Is a concise expression of the new institution.

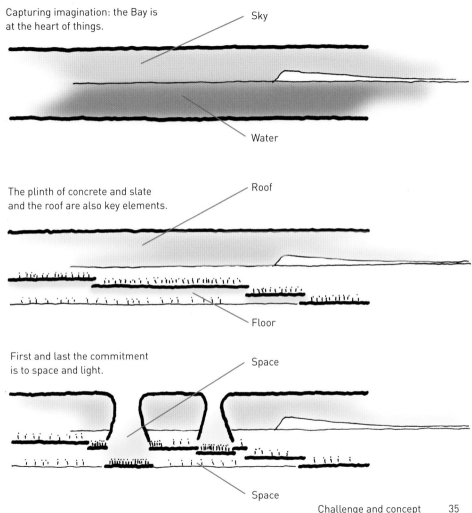

Capturing imagination: the Bay is at the heart of things.

Sky

Water

The plinth of concrete and slate and the roof are also key elements.

Roof

Floor

First and last the commitment is to space and light.

Space

Space

Ivan Harbour

Ivan Harbour, the Richard Rogers partner responsible for the Senedd, joined the practice in 1985. He started with the Lloyd's of London building in the City and later led the design of the European Court of Human Rights at Strasbourg, 1995, and the Bordeaux Law Courts, 1998. He developed his expertise in directing a variety of complex projects, insisting on a clear logic in every construction. His experience and perspective are world-wide.

Projects designed and built under his supervision include Terminal 4 at Barajas Airport, Madrid, which won the 2006 Stirling Prize, and Maggie's Centre at Charing Cross Hospital, the Stirling Prize winner in 2009. He led the design for the Antwerp Law Courts, affordable housing at Oxley Woods in Milton Keynes, the Barangaroo Masterplan, Sydney, and buildings in Washington, Qatar, Stuttgart, Taiwan, Seoul, Kyoto and Tokyo, among many others. He became a senior director at Richard Rogers in 1998. The practice's change of name to Rogers Stirk Harbour + Partners in 2007 recognised the contribution of Graham Stirk and Ivan Harbour. Following the death of Richard Rogers, the practice was again renamed as RSHP from 2022.

'figures are easy, aspiration
more complicated'

How I see it: Ivan Harbour's first rough outline for his colleagues: roof, floor, and distinctive light and air funnels in embryonic form.

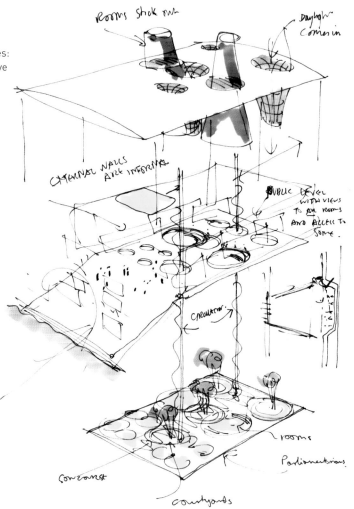

rooms stick out

Daylight comes in

EXTERNAL WALLS ARE INFORMAL

PUBLIC LEVEL WITH VIEWS TO 5TH ROOMS AND ACCESS TO SOME.

CIRCULATION

CONCOURSE

courtyards

rooms

Parliamentarians

Above the roof: south-west view from Tŷ Hywel across the Bay.

Lord Callaghan characterized the winning proposal as: 'Simple, elegant, economic, a gem ... It has the potential of becoming a great building, one of the most instantly recognizable pieces of architecture at the dawn of the twenty-first century'.

The project was always close to Richard Rogers's heart. Few architects number a parliament among their achievements. The Senedd was his firm's first pavilion building, the first to use timber on a large scale and the first with such a comprehensive commitment to sustainability.

The Senedd was an element of Britain's second-largest regeneration project, the thirteen-year renewal of 2,700 acres of dockland by the Cardiff Bay Development Corporation. In January 2000 the Assembly paid a nominal £1 for the land and while building was under construction Assembly Members debated in a temporary chamber in Crickhowell House. The Queen had opened the Assembly here in 1999 and spoke of 'a bridge into the future ... a forum in which all the people of this ancient and noble land will have a more resonant and democratic voice'.

Let there be light: early south-west view
towards Penarth with the idea of three funnels.

As sometimes happens with high-profile architecture, controversy came with the concrete. In July 2001 the Assembly stopped the project and recommissioned it two years later with Taylor Woodrow Construction as contractor and with Lord Rogers retained as architect. Although security considerations and questions of disabled access made changes in the construction inevitable, the Assembly stayed firmly with the original Rogers vision of space and light.

The Senedd was completed at a cost of £67 million and the Queen inaugurated it on Saint David's Day 2006. She and the Prince of Wales addressed Assembly Members and others in the Siambr. In a spirit of friendship and tradition the parliament of New South Wales presented the Assembly with a ceremonial mace.

Below: Under construction: the roof is in place; the Neuadd, the main hall, takes shape; steps lead to the Oriel level.

Below: Warm words: an early drawing shows sunlight reaching the chamber through the funnel lantern. Air rises and escapes through vents and through the funnel. The wind over the roof acts on the rudderlike fin and the cowl turns, warm air escaping on the lee side.

The Assembly, steered to completion by Richard Rogers and Ivan Harbour, met the challenge of 1998 and the Assembly's brief. The Siambr, for example, has a non-confrontational layout in preference to the Westminster model. The Assembly was obliged to promote sustainable development and its futuristic energy-saving practices would delight Scrooge. It is by no means a large construction, is neither monumental nor dominating, and avoids being 'openly adversarial in shape or argument'. Its quality is clear. It mixes panache with dignity and fulfils the hope that it would become an unmistakable banner of Wales. The camera loves it and its front-page image is memorable.

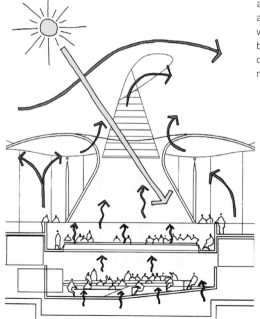

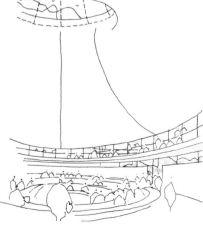

Skeletal elegance:
the Senedd takes shape.

Beautiful bones: the dramatic steel construction of the funnel over the debating chamber.

05 Red hot in Cardiff

The last shipload of coal departed Cardiff's West Dock in 1964. The final cargo left the East Dock six years later. The age Bute made had run its course. The majestic red Pierhead Building seemed suddenly stranded by the tide. By 1980 Cardiff docks were virtually derelict.

On William Frame's drawing board the Pierhead grew as a masterly flourish, brimming with late Victorian confidence. On the day the building opened in 1897 bosses wasted no time on ceremony: the doors opened and staff streamed straight to their desks, the clerks and assistants to work on ledgers and invoices, the senior men with important moustaches to make managerial decisions.

The Pierhead commanded the world's greatest coal port and from their offices the general manager and dockmaster ruled as gods. But they themselves were driven by the clock. And the tide called the tune. Business depended on rapid turnaround and swift departure.

Tour de force: a grand porch, an oriel bay window, arched top lights, steeply-pitched roofs, battlements, ornate chimneys – and gargoyles for fun.

Pierhead splendour: triple chimney stack, crenellated clock tower and a polygon bay with candle-snuffer roof.

Long trains of railway wagons carried coal to the waiting ships. Thousands of hauliers, weighers, trimmers and tippers filled the bunkers. Their clothes grew black with dust. Incoming cargoes of Scandinavian building wood and pit props added a timbery tang to smoke and steam.

Although steam was king the age of sail was enjoying its long last waltz. Cardiff bristled with the masts of coasters and oceangoing windships. The Royal Navy and commercial shipping relied for fuel on more than 150 coaling stations throughout the world – Aden, Ascension, Fiji, Trincomalee among them – and many of these were supplied by sailing vessels.

William Frame was architect to the third marquess of Bute and the Pierhead is considered his masterpiece. It cost £30,000, equivalent to about £3 million today. Like Cardiff Castle and the storybook fortress of Castell Coch it reflects Lord Bute's passion for the architectural exuberance popularized by Augustus Pugin in the parliament at Westminster.

Watching the ships come in: tramp steamer enters the West Dock, tea-time by the Pierhead clock.

Look up as you enter: decoration of the porch.

Below: 'Willum' – caricature of architect William Frame by Fred Weekes.

Frame added French accents to the Pierhead's Gothic style. He chose startling red-as-sunset brickwork, fired from the local Etruria Marl clay by J C Edwards at Ruabon, near Wrexham, and matched it with Edwards's handmade glazed terracotta tiles. These were imitations of coloured earthenware favoured in the Mediterranean and called majolica, from Maiolica, the Italian name for Majorca. Many architects chose the bold red bricks and tiles for civic buildings, libraries, colleges and hospitals.

The Pierhead's clock tower stages an elaborate entertainment of battlements, lions' heads, heraldic ornament, friezes, foliage and gargoyle spouts. Domed turrets flank the entrance arch. A company coat of arms, illustrated with a hybrid sail-and-steam ship and a railway locomotive, features on an exterior wall. The motto Wrth ddŵr a thân – By water and fire – salutes the steam revolution. A mosaic on the floor of the grand arcaded hall repeats the emblem and motto. The supporting columns are fluted and tiled. Daylight pours through immense windows. The magisterial granite staircase has a green glazed handrail, formidable newels and splendid Minton-style wall tiles.

Frame also designed the building's four clock faces. William Potts of Leeds built the clock mechanism which was replaced in 1973 by an electric movement. A collector in Birmingham, Alabama, bought the original drive in 1976 and sold it to Cardiff council in 2005. A Royal Welsh Regiment fanfare welcomed it back to the city. The original one-tonne bell is still in the tower, but is no longer struck.

Left: The Pierhead's southern
side; terracotta coat of arms;
main staircase.

Beware of the beasts:
gargoyles and little dragons.

Left: Control tower with fireplace: the chief dock manager's domain.

Right: Nothing left under-decorated; a fireplace fish.

The Pierhead building opened at the time the Bute Docks Company changed its name to the Cardiff Railway Company, the better to attract investors. A roll of honour on the ground floor lists the names of employees who served in the First World War. Black mourning stars mark the names of men killed.

Upstairs the chief dock manager's room is in Scottish baronial style with walnut panelling and a grandstand window overlooking the docks and harbour. We have to imagine it teeming with ships and men. The room's ceiling plasterwork is rich with oak leaves. The turreted and canopied terracotta fireplace is populated with carvings of fish and parrots and small birds peeping from leaves, the playful detail William Frame and Lord Bute enjoyed. The assistant dock manager used the grand room next door, and the dockmaster, too, had a commanding view from his ground floor office.

During the Second World War the Luftwaffe used the Pierhead as a target landmark. The building was later used by Associated British Ports and in 1998 it became a National Assembly for Wales property. Around £700,000 was spent on its renovation. With its galleries and lecture spaces it is both the Senedd visitor centre and a guide to Cardiff's maritime story. It is Grade I listed inside and out.

William Frame had worked as assistant to William Burges, Lord Bute's architect, on the restoration of Cardiff Castle and Castell Coch. He succeeded him when Burges died in 1881. Frame's drinking tried the patience of his tolerant employer. The marquess sacked him in 1890 but feeling he had acted harshly to a hard-working man he reinstated him. There was no rancour between the two. The marquess died in 1900 and in his will left Frame £1,000, equivalent to more than £90,000 today. Frame died six years later. His artistry entertains us still.

The Pierhead as storyteller: places where dock clerks and managers worked are now spaces for lectures, screens and exhibitions.

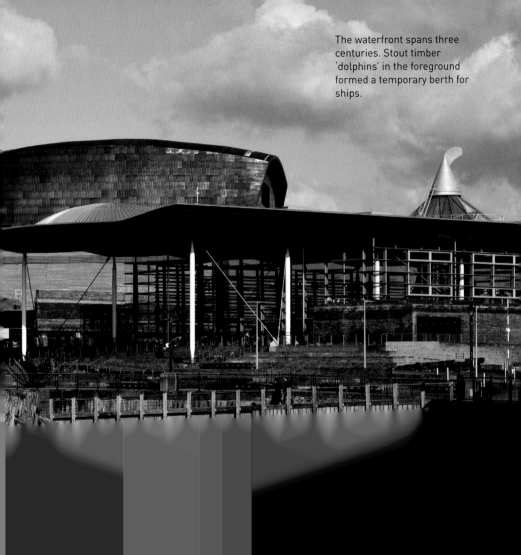

The waterfront spans three centuries. Stout timber 'dolphins' in the foreground formed a temporary berth for ships.

06 Senedd

In the ascent to the Senedd from the Bay the nineteenth century leads the way to the twenty-first. Steps from the waterfront boardwalk begin at the sandstone portal of the old East Dock. Over the years the warps and cables of countless ships sawed furrows into the curved brown walls.

Begun in 1852 the dock was four-fifths of a mile long when completed in 1859. The steps to the Senedd climb through part of the original sea lock where massive timber gates held back the water. The lock and the basin beyond were filled in during the 1970s and 1980s, and we have to imagine the traffic of ships where the Senedd rises today.

The building's refreshing simplicity of style completes a varied set of neighbours. The team includes the vivid Pierhead Building, the chelonian Wales Millennium Centre and the sharp-edged Atradius insurance offices. A short walk to the south the charming white Norwegian church plays mascot.

As the steps emerge from the dock the poignant memorial to seafarers lost in the Second World War is on the right. The Senedd flies the flags of the Welsh Parliament, Wales, and the United Kingdom. The steps meld with the tiers and terraces of the Senedd's defining plinth.

Poised: symbol of modern Wales.

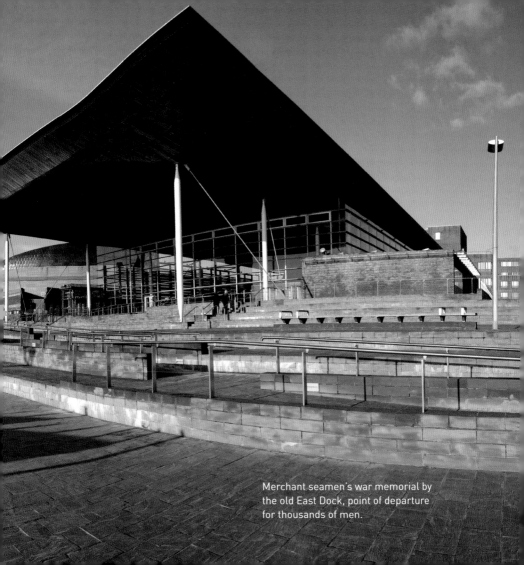

Merchant seamen's war memorial by the old East Dock, point of departure for thousands of men.

Blue-grey slate cladding hewn from Cwt-y-Bugail quarry near Blaenau Ffestiniog covers the concrete foundation base and lives harmoniously with the slate strata of the Millennium Centre. On the southern corner of the Senedd plinth a sculpted slate comma forms a sitting space.

At the threshold the drama is in close-up and we are drawn into it. The roof soars high above the slate terrace rendezvous, a sheltering portico poised on slender steel bodkins – a bold veranda, a curving wing, a shading shamiana: whatever we wish. The spectacle never palls. The floating roof and handsome slate flooring are both inside and outside the inviting glass pavilion. The low-iron glass throughout the structure is of startling clarity.

Unity: sliced slate from the quarry, glass and Welsh steel from the furnace, cedar from the forest.

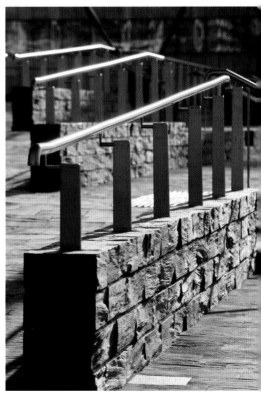

A key part of the architectural drama, the 'floating' wing-like roof, seen against the Millennium Centre's coppery shell.

Below: Enduring rock: slate from the quarry.

The 'Assembly Field' glass sculpture created by Danny Lane on the Senedd's west side. Five parallel rows of thirty-two splinter-proof elements of varying heights rise on a hexagonal grid and form a wind shelter, changing appearance as the viewer moves past or around them.

Broad slate steps lead from the Neuadd to the Oriel, the upper level and cafe, another space for gatherings, recitals and exhibitions. Chairs and tables are stylish and unshowy. Up here we feel a more intimate involvement with the masterpiece cedar ceiling. The curves and the six shapely oval hollows were computer-sculpted to combine delicacy with strength. A concealed steel framework of 420 tonnes supports the ceiling from above and slim steel columns from below, an amazing show.

Light and shade: the view from the MSs' gallery above the Oriel.

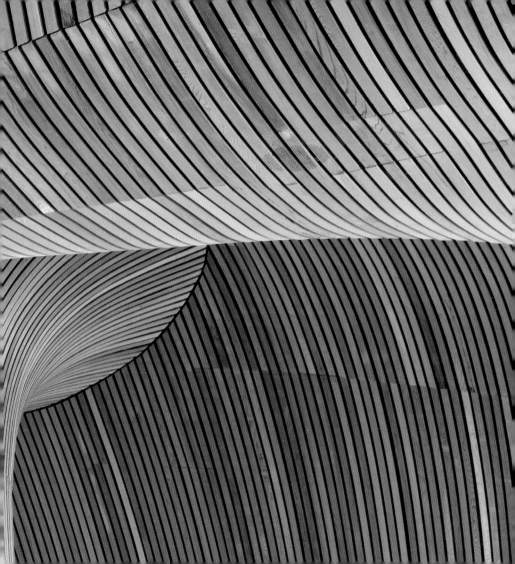

Walk in the wood: fragrant Canadian cedar curved for contemplation.

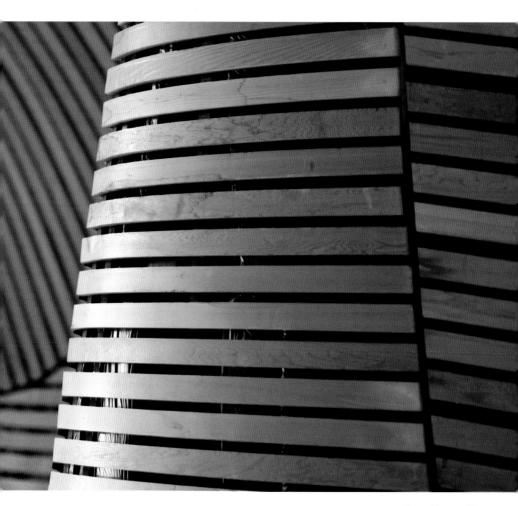

The glass circle.

The emblematic funnel, clearly visible from outside the building, was in the first shorthand design doodle and ascends theatrically to the starlit timber-strip heavens. Where it meets the Oriel floor a glass circle allows the public the democratic pleasure of looking past their toes to their elected representatives below.

The Siambr's public gallery
with seats for 128, including
press and wheelchair space.

Lantern and mirror, harnessing light.

Right: Oak desks, oak floor and pin-drop acoustics.

The funnel breaks through the roof line and emerges into the open. Its crucial double function is to illuminate and ventilate the Siambr. Look up from the Siambr or its public gallery and there is the sky. A conical skylight-lantern directs natural light through the bell of the funnel. An ingenious conical mirror in the funnel's throat reflects and enhances light and is raised and lowered according to need. Within the funnel an array of eighty-nine horizontal aluminium rings enhance and diffuse the natural lighting.

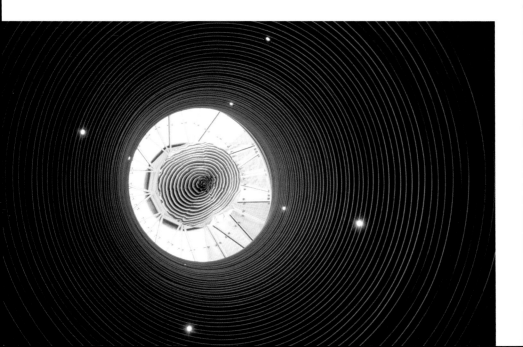

Sunshine bell and the
clear light of day.

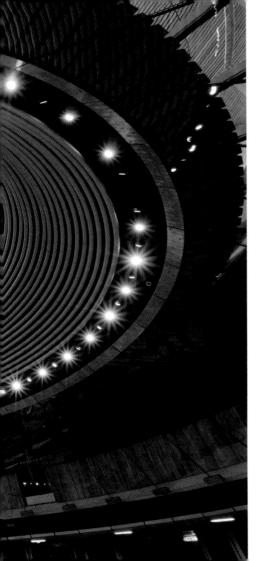

Atop the lantern a cowl, nearly twenty feet tall, turns as a weathervane with the wind, its fin like a pavilion flag. Negative pressure on the lee side draws warm air out of the Siambr, as through a chimney. Traditional oast-houses dry their hops in much the same way.

The red light glows and the speaker has the floor.

Smash hit: Swansea-based Alexander Beleschenko made the 'Heart of Wales' sculpture by bonding layers of glass, smashing and reforming them in a mould to create a light-capturing surface illustrating a theme of emergence.

Green, white and red

During debates and business in the Siambr the sixty Members of the Senedd use nineteen-inch touch screens served by a unique custom-built computer system. This is simplified and stripped of any function that is not useful.

An agenda displays all the information needed for a day's business. Chamber services provide onscreen documents relevant to proceedings so that MSs can work without paper. The MS's desk doubles as a lectern and is fitted with a drawer.

MSs use an instant messaging system to send individual notes to fellow-members or a group message to those in their own party. This function is especially useful to party whips at voting time. The messaging system does not work outside the chamber and none of its data is recorded or saved.

An MS touches a screen symbol to alert the Llywydd, the Presiding Officer, that he or she wishes to speak in a debate. An engineer in the sound gallery switches on the microphone when the MS is called to speak. If the speaker overruns an allotted time the Llywydd has the option of pressing a red button to switch off the microphone. Computer boxes in the MSs' desks are silent, fan-less and make little heat. If a box malfunctions the MS moves to a spare desk and

staff carry out a swift 'pit-change' and replace the box in a few minutes.

The electronic voting system is as perfect as possible and works independently of the rest of the information technology system. An MS must be in the chamber to cast a vote. To do so he or she presses one of three buttons, green, white or red, on the right beneath the screen. Green is Yes, white is Abstain, red is No. A fourth option is not to vote at all. A brief interval allows for a change of mind. When the vote is open the Presiding Officer sees on his screen what is happening, although MSs cannot.

As well as a mailbox for messages within the chamber each MS has access to email and the Internet. Letters and speeches can be written onscreen. There is a spellcheck and a calculator. MSs view short DVD presentations on the four Siambr screens. Proceedings are transmitted by Senedd.tv within the Senedd and Tŷ Hywel and can be seen live and without charge online. The BBC, ITV and S4C, with studios in Tŷ Hywel, also receive live pictures for use in their news programmes. Television cameras recessed in the chamber perimeter are directed from a studio in Tŷ Hywel. Two of them are fixed and six move discreetly and silently on rails.

The public gallery accommodates 128 spectators in seating that puts some people in mind of a nonconformist chapel. There is easy access for twelve wheelchairs. A press conference room is nearby. Like the MSs the public can hear the simultaneous translation of Welsh into English. Similar facilities for spectators are available in the three committee rooms on the ground floor. These rooms and offices are in courtyards, or canyons, cut into the foundation plinth on either side of the Siambr, and all have glass walls facing into the courtyards in keeping with the theme of transparency and natural light. Their smooth grey concrete walls are gently enhanced by Martin Richman's fabric acoustic panels, painted in shades of green, yellow and pink. More glass-fronted rooms accommodate party meetings, and the MSs' tea room dispenses calming cups. Members and officials reach the Senedd by way of two glass bridges from Tŷ Hywel.

News on the move: reporters gather for a press conference in the Senedd.

Around 600 sound-proofing panels, timber frames covered with acoustically-neutral fabric, are installed throughout the Senedd. Martin Shipman painted about 270 of them, creating a unique set for each location, the designs suggesting rock strata and mineral deposits, the source of the character, culture and wealth of Wales.

Glazed walls in meeting rooms and committee rooms facing internal courtyards continue the theme of transparency.

Australian salute

The mace presented to the Senedd at the opening ceremony in 2006 celebrates a namesake link with Wales dating from James Cook's exploration of Australia's east coast in 1770. A belief that New South Wales owes its name to a supposed resemblance between the Australian and Welsh coasts is mistaken. During the first of his three Pacific voyages Cook surveyed 2,000 miles of Australia's east coast and took possession of it on 22 August. As an explorer and geographer Cook had a duty to name places but he gave no name to the coast at that time. New England, New Britain and Nova Scotia were, of course, already taken. It was October when Cook inserted the name New Wales into his August journal entry. His companion Joseph Banks noted in his own journal: 'New Wales bestowed by Cook.' But Cook perhaps forgot, and then remembered, that there was already a New Wales in Canada. In subsequent copies of his journal South was inserted into New Wales. The land he explored was not named Australia until 1803. The northern part of New South Wales became Queensland in 1853.

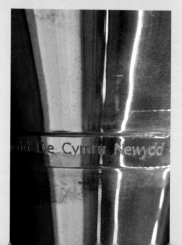

The mace, fashioned from brass, silver and gold, lies in a recess in the Presiding Officer's desk in the Siambr. A mace is the mystical symbol of the Speaker's authority in parliament. The House of Commons has perpetuated tradition by presenting maces to several Commonwealth legislatures.

Footnote to history: shared name, shared heritage.

07 A smaller bill

From the beginning the Senedd design brief committed architects and builders to a well-behaved building of the future, lean and green in its consumption of heat, light, electrical power, water and materials. It was designed for a life of at least a century and intended to be a pioneer in sustainable construction and use. Resources were to be enhanced rather than depleted.

Only in a new building could these aims and obligations be achieved. The Assembly is the first political body in Britain obliged to promote such development.

The commitment is to let nature do as much work as possible through fresh air ventilation, natural light, heat from the earth, rainwater flushing and the use of cheap wood-waste fuel for heating. The target is to reduce running costs by a third to a half.

It was decidedly more practical to consider a new building as a whole, to wire in computer technology and to plan for the long term. Carpet, for example, would have been a cheaper floor covering than the slate so widely used in the building, but over 100 years would prove far more costly and difficult to maintain.

We start with the foundations. The reinforced concrete base is blast-resistant and absorbs some of the wind pressure from the building. It radiates coolness in warm weather and saves energy by moderating temperature fluctuations. In some places the concrete is left exposed because of the pleasing appearance of its high-quality soft grey finish.

Heating and cooling of the Senedd are achieved largely through renewable energy, the constant warm temperature of the earth. Heat is moved rather than created by burning oil or gas. Twenty-seven boreholes of eighteen inches diameter are sunk through the foundation to a depth of 330 feet where the earth temperature is 16C/64F.

In winter heat is drawn to the surface through insulated Alkathene piping and transferred to exchangers to provide the Senedd's underfloor heating. In summer the system is reversed: heat is moved from the Senedd into the ground and there is no need for energy-hungry chillers.

This economical geothermal system ensures that primary energy consumption and emissions are reduced. Most new houses in Sweden are fitted with it and although it is more expensive to install initially the bills in the long term are 30-40 per cent smaller.

Engine room: tapping the earth for warmth, and the hot water buffer tank for the earth heat exchanger.

Cool Cymru: a Senedd technician adjusts climate control valves. Thermal covers prevent condensation.

The Senedd's bright red boiler heats water for hand washing and for heating convectors. It consumes biomass fuel of wood pellets or wood chips, usually offcuts and furniture scrap, and is virtually carbon-neutral. In winter it burns fifteen tons in two and a half to three weeks, and is switched off from April to October.

As well as illuminating the Siambr and committee rooms natural light reaches the heart of the building by way of light wells. Artificial lights in committee rooms and offices have computer identities and are controlled by sensors programmed to maintain illumination at 500 lux as natural light dims or brightens. Infrared sensors monitor movement in the rooms and if none is detected in twenty minutes lights are automatically switched off.

Ventilation is chiefly natural and operates through almost all parts of the building. Automatic controls open vents on opposite walls to create air currents. Air is also introduced through floor inlets and escapes through roof vents or controlled windows. Air conditioning has been eliminated from most of the building but is available in the Siambr and committee rooms. A unique system draws air from the outside and passes it through a frost coil and then through filters into the building.

Rainwater, known as grey water, is collected on the Senedd's roof and funnelled directly into two 50,000-litre tanks at ground level. Treated with chemicals and ultra-violet light to destroy bacteria, it flushes lavatories and greatly reduces water demand. Rainwater falls in such abundance on the roof that some of it is dumped.

The innovative environmental features in the Senedd have earned an Excellent BREEAM (Building Research Establishment Environmental Assessment Method) certification, the highest achievable.

08

In conversation with Richard Rogers and Ivan Harbour

'It's difficult for the architect to say what's successful. The users are more important at this point. But this building in Cardiff Bay lifts my spirits. There are certain buildings amongst one's works with which one has a more passionate relationship than others. The Senedd is one of them.'

Richard Rogers (1933-2021) was a leading international architect for more than fifty years.

Ivan Harbour joined Richard Rogers in 1985 and was project director for the Senedd building from 1998-2005.

Lord Rogers and Ivan Harbour talked to Trevor Fishlock at the Rogers Stirk Harbour + Partners building by the Thames near Hammersmith Bridge.

In conversation with Richard Rogers and Ivan Harbour 139

RR: Architecture is about improving the quality of life. We thought hard about the concept of democracy as an exchange of ideas and the Assembly as a democratic meeting place, a microcosm of a city. Its transparency is critical. People should be able to see what their government does. Here is a place where you learn about democracy and democracy is not hidden. It is full of light, looks at the sky and the sea, looks outwards.

IH: The Assembly wished for something inspirational, the future rather than the symbols of the past. The brief was in two parts and one of them was an introduction of a few paragraphs by Lord Callaghan. His was the aspirational side to the brief. And that's what we needed to see. Figures are quite easy, but aspiration and how you communicate it is far more complicated. His words were subtle. He didn't say he wanted a building that would shout. He dared to imagine that if the building

were successful, if it really worked well for Wales, it would come to be associated with the country. That was the challenge. Without it this building wouldn't exist as it is. It owes a lot to Jim Callaghan.

RR: We like to inspire.

IH: Most of our work comes from competitions. Some competitions are badly run, people ask too much, but the Assembly's was very well run under the auspices of the Royal Institute of British Architects. It wanted key information, not the fine detail, allowing us to concentrate on getting the concept across. We suggested that the Assembly should occupy all of the space up to the adjoining buildings, the Pierhead and the yet-to-be-constructed Wales Millennium Centre. Hats off to the Assembly: they realized they had to be bigger than the site defined by the parcelling out of land to businesses moving to Cardiff Bay. Obviously the Senedd was more important than that.

'the building adds to your knowledge as you progress with it'

RR: We often say that architecture grows out of constraints. We are not abstract artists. The art is in taking constraints, turning them upside down and developing something that emerges to your advantage. It is difficult to work on a completely clear site. You need those pressures.

IH: A greenfield site is a problem because there's nothing to respond to or push against.

RR: It's a mistake to think the architect does not want any constraints, and also to think that he knows exactly what the building is going to look like from his drawings. He doesn't: the building adds to your knowledge as you progress with it. It's always changing. A client once asked: Why didn't you tell me it was going to look like that? I said: Because I didn't really know. The point I was trying to make is you don't see it all. However good the models are there will be certain areas where you are taken by surprise, certain areas where you make decisions quite late on the juxtaposition of things. There's something wrong if you approach a building with complete pre-conceived ideas.

IH: The great joy for me in architecture is not quite knowing what a building is going to be like, but being pleasantly surprised that it's what you imagined it might be.

RR: The two key parts of any project are a good brief and a good client who guides and gets involved. It's better to have a client say No rather than I don't know. Don't know is difficult to work with. The ability to be able to argue about things is a better way. If it's rational there's always another way of doing it. Looking back, I think the more interesting buildings are those in which the client had a real role.

IH: One of the special features of this building is what you don't see, and that comes from the Assembly's commitment to sustainable development. This is the first building that we've been involved in as a practice devoted so broadly to sustainability.

RR: I've been interested in sustainability for a long time. This is a really modern building, one of the most sustainable we have ever designed. Most of the space has natural ventilation.

IH: Conceptually it's a democratic cover. The form of the roof developed from our aim to get the lightest structure that would sit on very fine columns and seemed to float as much as possible. It is essentially a flat roof and the undulation gives it a human scale as well as rigidity. The funnel emerged because the building essentially had no sides. The inspiration for it all came from the water as a surface, which would be the public surface, with the sky essentially being the roof. The key point, the meeting of the elected and the electorate, is symbolized by drawing the sky down to the earth. All these ideas have more than one point of origin.

RR: I don't think one has these things ready on a mental shelf, but one certainly stores ideas in one's mind all the time, and they go on maturing for years.

IH: That's the subconscious the computer doesn't have, fortunately. Architects know a little about a lot, and we need to work with people who know a lot about a little. So we operate with many consultants, real specialists.

'inspiration came from the water and the sky'

How you create, how you solve those problems – that's something you can't write down. If you could you'd be wealthy. I've been working with Richard for twenty-five years and I remain excited about tomorrow. It's a creative environment.

RR: I am as passionate about architecture today as I was when I was a young man. Of course it's nice to have prizes, but you can't really go by criticisms or prizes. In the end you have to believe in a building.

IH: Building the Senedd was fraught at times. There was a point where we weren't working on the job, and we re-tendered for it, to get it back. When we delivered the scheme we weren't asked to produce a model, but we elected to make one, and that in the end sold it to everyone. For me it's a success, a place built in the spirit we originally tabled, expressing the spirit Jim Callaghan was after. I feel we may have answered his words in a way that would make him proud.

RR: In our organisation participation is rooted in the way we work. The firm is not me, it's a team. On Mondays we have a forum and everybody comes to discuss the designs, four or five projects, including clients, engineers and others.

IH: Everyone there offers experience and opinion. Our role as architects is to deal with these inputs and create something.

RR: It's difficult for the architect to say what's successful. The users are more important at this point. But this building in Cardiff Bay lifts my spirits. There are certain buildings amongst one's works with which one has a more passionate relationship than others. The Senedd is one of them.

In the mind's eye: imagining the Senedd.

Lord Rogers of Riverside

Richard Rogers (1933-2021) was a leading and influential international architect for over fifty years, a champion of city regeneration and public spaces. He understood architecture as a social art whose purpose is to enhance city life. His designs reflect his deep interest in adaptable, flexible and sustainable constructions.

He was knighted in 1991 and created a life peer in 1996. In 1995 he was the first architect to deliver the BBC Reith Lectures. His subject was 'Cities for a Small Planet'.

He was born in Florence in 1933, deriving his English surname from an ancestor who had settled in Venice. His parents fled fascism and moved to Britain when he was five. He won a scholarship to Yale, returned to Britain and set up a practice with Norman Foster. Later he and Renzo Piano found fame as creators of the controversial Centre Pompidou in Paris, completed in 1977, the year he started the Richard Rogers Partnership. By the 1980s he was among the top three British architects. He was a Royal Academician in 1984 and winner of the Royal Institute of British Architects Gold Medal in 1985. France awarded him the Légion d'Honneur in 1986.

The British government appointed Lord Rogers chairman of its Urban Task Force on the state of cities in 1998. He was awarded the Thomas Jefferson Memorial Foundation Medal for Architecture in 1999, the Golden Lion for Lifetime Achievement at the Venice Biennale in 2006 and the Pritzker Architecture Prize in 2007. He became a Member of the Order of the Companions of Honour in 2008.

09

Democracy road 1832–2005

The 1832 Reform Act extended the vote from the landed gentry to middle-class men of property, giving political importance to industrial towns. It left the gentry and nobility dominating parliament and working people embittered.

The 1867 Reform Act responded to working-class pressure and broadened the vote. But it enfranchised only one third of men, excluded women and did not create democracy on a large scale.

The 1884 Reform Act filled some of the 1867 gaps, extended the vote to the countryside but left many disfranchised with an electorate of 5.6 million in a population of 36 million.

The 1918 Representation of the People Act enlarged the vote to all men over twenty-one and to women over thirty who paid rates or were ratepayers' wives.

The 1928 Representation of the People Act included women over twenty-one in the electorate.

The 1948 Representation of the People Act abolished the university vote and the right of people to vote both where they lived and where they had business.

The 1969 Representation of the People Act gave the vote to people over eighteen and increased the electorate to 40 million.

In 1973 the Royal Commission on the Constitution under Lord Kilbrandon recommended assemblies for Wales and Scotland.

In the 1979 referendums Wales and Scotland rejected devolution proposals. In 1997 they approved them.

The Government of Wales Act 1998 created the National Assembly for Wales, now the Welsh Parliament. In the first election in May 1999 women won twenty-four of the sixty seats. In the second election in 2005 women won twenty-eight.

10 Artwork and artists

Richard Harris of Builth Wells shaped thirty-nine slate stones to form his meeting place on the Senedd plinth.

Brian Fell created the Merchant Seafarers' War Memorial dedicated in 1997 to the men who sailed from Cardiff, Penarth and Barry, 1939-45, and never returned. Louise Shenstone and Adrian Butler made the accompanying mosaic.

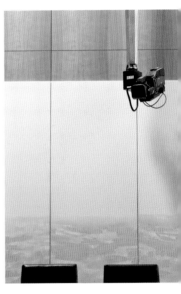

Danny Lane, an American
sculptor, created
the 'Assembly Field'
sculpture, five parallel
rows of thick glass.

Alexander Beleschenko
designed the glass sculpture in
the Siambr. It is two metres in
diameter and lit from below.

Martin Richman designed the
acoustic panels in committee
rooms.

11 Writing Squad poems

Academi, the society of writers in Wales, founded Young People's Writing Squads to encourage children to write and to work with established authors. Fifty-eight young writers spent a day at the Senedd with their tutors and here are two of the poems they composed:

The Senedd

The ceiling reminds me of veins
Flowing with blood, free and full of life.
It stands so proud
Making it feel so real, so alive.
The Chamber is the heart
Where women and men sit and debate
Helping Wales grow stronger as a country
So the world will sing its praise.
The floor black and simple
But means so much
It carries the heritage of our country
As we carry our bodies along it
The magnificent glass is like eyes
Opening the Bay and letting nature in
The magic, the dreams, the wonder
That leaves its mark in every heart.

Lauren Slye, 13
Rhondda Cynon Taf Writing Squad

Y Senedd

Yn y Bae mae'n Senedd ninnau
fel madarchen bren dan wydrau.
Seddi'r Siambr sy'n rhesymu,
botwm sgrin sy'n penderfynu.

Yn y gwydr gwelwn ddadlau,
yn y pren, fe glywn y pleidiau'n
cynrychioli ac yn craffu,
a chreu cyfraith er mwyn Cymru.

Y mae'r wlad a'r dre yn siffrwd
yn llawn cyffro dan ei nenfwd.
Ar y llawr cawn wylio gobaith
yn y llechi'n gwawrio eilwaith.

Uwch y Senedd y mae newid,
yn yr awyr y mae rhyddid
fel y môr o amgylch Cymru
weithiau'n sibrwd, weithiau'n gweiddi.

Yn y Bae mae llais y bobol,
ac mae cychod ein dyfodol;
yn yr haul mae hawliau'n bloeddio,
yn y dŵr mae fory'n sgleinio.

Sgwad Sgwennu Caerdydd: Gwenllian Davies,
Broni Koziel, Lauren Moore, Elisa Morris,
Ela Pari-Huws, Megan Rose, Greta Siôn
(pawb yn 14) a Ceri Wyn Jones.

Build facts

The specifics of the brief included the stipulation that the building be an exemplar for access, that sustainable strategies and renewable energy systems be implemented throughout, that the building have a minimum 100-year life span, and that, wherever possible, Welsh materials be used.

Other elements included a 610 square metre (6,566 sq ft) debating chamber for sixty to eighty members, three committee rooms, offices, a media briefing room, tea room, members' lounge, public galleries, and a main hall to act as reception, orientation and exhibition space. At Rogers Stirk Harbour + Partners suggestion, the site, which is located directly facing Cardiff Bay, was expanded to take advantage of the opportunity to complete the 'jigsaw' of development in the immediate vicinity and to create an important new public space for the city.

Client: National Assembly for Wales

Area: Gross internal area: 5,308 m²

Construction cost: £67,000,000

Architect: Rogers Stirk Harbour + Partners

Team: David Ardill, Stephen Barret, Ed Burgess, Mike Davies, Lucy Evans, Mike Fairbrass, Rowena Fuller, Marco Goldschmied, Ivan Harbour, Mimi Hawley, Kazu Kofuku, Tom Lacy, James Leathem, Jose Llerena, John Lowe, Tim Mason, Stephen McKaeg, Annie Miller, Liz Oliver, Tamiko Onozawa, Mathis Osterhage, Andrew Partridge, Inma Pedragosa, Tosan Popo, Richard Rogers, Simon Smithson, Neil Wormsley, Daniel Wright, Yoshi Uchiyama, John Young

Structural Engineer: Arup

Environmental Consultant: BDSP Partnership

Contractor: Taylor Woodrow Construction

Project Managers: Schal

Landscaping: Gillespies

Fire Engineering: Warrington Fire Research

Acoustics: Sound Research Laboratories

Access: Vin Goodwin Access Consultant

Broadcasting Consultant: Department Purple

Wind Engineering: Arup

Lift Consultant: Arup

Facade Engineering: Arup

Bomb Blast: TPS consult

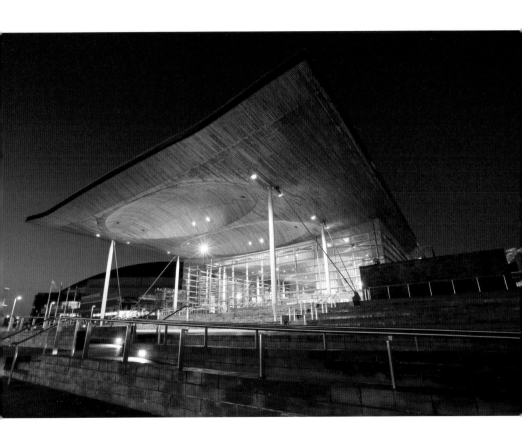

Acknowledgements

Architects illustrations courtesy of Rogers Stirk Harbour + Partners, pages 32/33, 35, 38, 40/41, 43.

Aerial view page 6, photography Simon Regan/ Photolibrarywales.

Cardiff Bay aerial page 10/11, © Crown copyright (2010) Visit Wales.

Senedd Model page 144/145, © Eamon O'Mahony, photographer.

Aerial view of wind cowl page 39, and entrance lobby image page 42, © Grant Smith, photographer.

Roof and Debating Chamber under construction, pages 44/45 and 46/47, © Katsuhisa Kida, photographer.

Archive photographs courtesy of: Bute Archive at Mount Stuart, page 24; Cardiff County Council Library Service, page 19; Media Wales Limited, pages 26/27, 28; © National Maritime Museum, Greenwich, London, page 29; National Museum of Wales, pages 20/21, 22, 23, 25, 27, 30, 31, 51.

Archive research: Ami Zienkiewicz.

The author thanks Geraint Talfan Davies, Malcolm Parry, Iwan Williams and Penny Symon.

Senedd
Published in Great Britain in 2023 by Graffeg Limited.

Written by Trevor Fishlock copyright © 2010.
Photography by Andrew Molyneux copyright © 2010.
Designed and produced by Graffeg Limited copyright © 2023.

Large format editions first published by Graffeg 2010 © Copyright Graffeg 2010:
Paperback English ISBN 9781905582433
Hardback English ISBN 9781905582457
Paperback Welsh ISBN 9781905582440
Hardback Welsh ISBN 9781905582464

Graffeg Limited, 24 Stradey Park Business Centre, Mwrwg Road, Llangennech, Llanelli, Carmarthenshire, SA14 8YP, Wales, UK.
Tel: 01554 824000. www.graffeg.com.

Trevor Fishlock is hereby identified as the author of this work in accordance with section 77 of the Copyright, Designs and Patents Act 1988.

A CIP Catalogue record for this book is available from the British Library.

T211122

ISBN 9781913134853

1 2 3 4 5 6 7 8 9

MIX
Paper | Supporting responsible forestry
FSC® C016973
www.fsc.org